*L3*

*The Pond*

# The Pond

## (Revised Edition)

poems by
**Mervyn Morris**

New Beacon Books Ltd
London ● Port of Spain

First Published 1973
by New Beacon Books Ltd.,
76 Stroud Green Road.
London N4 3EN.

Revised edition published 1997.

ISBN 1873201 13 3

Printed by Villiers Publications Ltd.,
19 Sylvan Avenue,
London N3 2LE.

*for Helen*

# ACKNOWLEDGEMENTS

Acknowledgements are due to the following publications in which some of these poems have appeared: *The Sunday Gleaner, Public Opinion Annual, Jamaica Journal, Caribbean Quarterly, Savacou, Bim, The Literary Half-Yearly, English, Outposts,* and *The Times Literary Supplement.*

## REVISED EDITION

*The Pond* was first published in 1973. This is a revised edition. The notes give details of the earlier version. Four of the poems have new titles.

# CONTENTS

# VALLEY PRINCE
*(for Don D.)*

Me one, way out in the crowd,
I blow the sounds, the pain,
but not a soul
would come inside my world
or tell me how it true.
I love a melancholy baby,
sweet, with fire in her belly;
and like a spite
the woman turn a whore.
Cool and smooth around the beat
she wake the note inside me
and I blow me mind.

Inside here, me one
in the crowd again,
and plenty people
want me blow it straight.
But straight is not the way; my world
don' go so; that is lie.
Oonoo gimme back me trombone, man:
is time to blow me mind.

# A READING °

Faraway eyes
indifferent as glass

Come with me come
inside the park
there is a fountain
at the centre

Eyes
at last eyes warm

pathways entice

Moving together
eyes holding eyes
we make a journey
both devise

Far
at the centre
the fountain

blooms

° See Notes, beginning p. 47.

# A FLOWER A WEED

he planted plenty seed°
but where he dropped
a flower a weed
would sprout

he pulled the weed out
sowed again
but where he urged
a flower weed came out

despairing
of the strangled flower
he let the dull weed grow
its awkward power

# GREATEST SHOW ON EARTH

The Great Majumboes
(to the noise of drums)
feign danger every show:
vivid above the safety nets
they swing.

The Mighty Marvo cracks the whip:
well-drugged tigers lumber into line.

Between the tigers and the acrobats
I do my act I
sit on chairs that aren't there
I play for time
(between the tigers and the acrobats)
a dwarf
who owns no whip
and will not leave this ground.

## STRIPPER

At a sleazy club where strippers are on view
a weary poet stopped for wine°
and song; but had to take the stripper too,
whose writhing seemed an image of his line.
She put on clothes to take them off, she wore
performing pieces, such a fuss she made
of skimpy little veils before
her parts (which never were displayed)!
Riddling hard to music, she performed
her teasing art, for which the patron paid.
Nice fleshy legs, gyrating hips that warmed
the watchers, sensuous lively educated tits.
The poet looked away, to check the eyes
of grim-faced lechers, soft men going to bits,
suckers deceived by lighting, sold on lies
(while there behind the smoke-dimmed crowd
the cunning pander lurked, a ponce on guard).
She took the last piece off the law allowed.
The poet felt his symbol growing hard.

# NURSERY

Everyone suddenly burst out screaming
and hurling plastic building-blocks;
the room was a riot of colour.

Did that autistic child have duller
things in mind, hugging his little box°
of bricks and quietly beaming?

# CATCH A NIGGER

At home with his creative curse
he lived inside; and (what was worse)
declined to share the public strain.
His beat was individual pain.°

The censors grew more angry and more loud:
how dare he set himself outside the crowd?
"The times are critical. You're either for
or you're against us. This is war!"

And then a man with an enormous head
assaulted him. The victim bled
outside, in open view. Perhaps the pack
would sniff his blood and classify it black?

"Fee fi fo fum,
When you perform, our god is dumb;
Eeny meeny miney mo,
You're a Nigger Minstrel Show!"

He stanched the public wound, and bled
inside again. His blood was red.

# TO AN EXPATRIATE FRIEND

Colour meant nothing. Anyone
who wanted help, had humour or was kind
was brother to you; categories of skin
were foreign; you were colour-blind.

And then the revolution. Black
and loud the horns of anger blew
against the long oppression; sufferers
cast off the precious values of the few.

New powers re-enslaved us all:
each person manacled in skin, in race.
You could not wear your paid-up dues;
the keen discriminators typed your face.

The future darkening, you thought it time
to say goodbye. It may be you were right.°
It hurt to see you go; but, more,
it hurt to see you slowly going white.

# I AM THE MAN

I am the man that build his house on shit
I am the man that watch you bulldoze it
I am the man of no fixed address
Follow me now

I am the man that have no job
I am the man that have no vote
I am the man that have no voice
Hear me now

I am the man that have no name
I am the man that have no home
I am the man that have no hope
Nothing is mine

I am the man that file the knife
I am the man that make the bomb
I am the man that grab the gun
Study me now

## TO THE UNKNOWN NON-COMBATANT

When the battle started
he was quick to duck.
He lay on his face in the open street
cursing his luck.

"Come join us!" (voices from the left)
"Come help us in the fight!"
"Be honest with yourself; you're ours,"
said voices from the right.

Meanwhile the bullets overhead
were troubling him somewhat
and buildings burning either side
had made the middle hot.

He thought perhaps he'd better choose.
He crawled to join a side.
A bullet clapped him in the neck —
Of course he died.

They left him face-down in the dust,
carcass going rotten.
Bullets whistled overhead.
He was forgotten.

# THE HOUSE-SLAVE

A drum thumps, faraway;
around the lamp my tribe of blood
are singing brothers home.

But soon that central fire will rage
too harsh for relics of the whip:
they'll burn this building,
fire these books, this art.

And these are my rooms now:
my pallid masters fled,
freeing the only home I knew.
I'll stay another night,
sounding my tutored terror of the dark.

# RASTA REGGAE
*(for The Mystics)*

out of that pain
that bondage
heavy heavy sounds
our brothers' weary march
our shackled trip

a joyful horn takes off
to freedom time
remembered & foretold°

Release I brother let me go
let my people go
home to Ethiopia
in the mind

# CASE-HISTORY, JAMAICA

In 19-something X was born
in Jubilee Hospital, howling, black.

In 19- (any date plus four)
X went out to school.
They showed him pretty pictures
of his Queen.

When he was seven, in elementary school, °
he asked what naygas were.
In secondary school he knew.
He asked in History one day
where slaves came from.
"Oh, Africa," the master said.
"Get on with your work."

Up at the university he didn't find himself;
and, months before he finally dropped out,
would ramble round the campus late at night
and daub his blackness on the walls.

# UNIVERSITY STUDY °

The window opened
on a tangled growth
of shrub.
He moved his wooden desk.

Second reel, New Life:
a barbed-wire fence
rough cobblestones
a solitary tree
and brown leaves
falling, falling.

He moved the damn desk back.
O brave new world:
incipient jungle
just outside.

He drew the curtains
and stayed in.
But all day long
the mind projected
images

one tree alone
self-strangled shrub
and brown leaves
falling free

# THE EARLY REBELS

Time and the changing passions played them tricks,
Killing the shop-soiled resolutions dead.
Gone are the early angry promises
Of rich men squeezed, of capitalists bled.
More adult honesties have straightened ties
And brushed the dinner-jackets clean,
Maturer minds have smelt out fallacies
And redefined what thinkers mean.

Hope drives a chromium symbol now
And smiles a toothpaste passion to the poor,
With colder eloquence explaining how
The young were foolish when they swore
They'd see those dunghills dank and dreary
All replaced by bright new flats:
Good sense was never youthful fury
And rash young promises by brats...

"Let's drink a loyal toast to dedication:
We mean the same but youth is past;
We are the fathers of our nation,
The thinking leaders come at last.
Cheers for the faith of simple minds,
Cheers for the love of humble friends;
Love does not alter when it finds
That we have redefined its ends."

# SATIRIST °

Satirical vision:
bloodshot eyes
darting derision,
laughing at lies.

When the eyes turn in
will the dry mind grin?
If the eyes talk true
will the heart laugh too?

If the eyes don't lie
will the dry mind cry?
If the eyes go deep
will the cold heart weep?

# THE DAY MY FATHER DIED

The day my father died
I could not cry;
My mother cried,
Not I.

His face on the pillow
In the dim light
Wrote mourning to me,
Black and white.

We saw him struggle,
Stiffen, relax;
The face fell empty,
Dead as wax.

I'd read of death
But never seen.
My father's face, I swear,
Was not serene.

Topple that lie,
However appealing:
That face was absence
Of all feeling.

My mother's tears were my tears,
Each sob shook me:
The pain of death is living,
The dead are free.

For me my father's death
Was mother's sorrow;
That day was her day,
Loss was tomorrow.

## TO A CRIPPLED SCHOOLMASTER

Your study doubled as a Common Room,
With billiards, laughter, loud debate;
And if some little cretin went too far
Your magisterial wit would set him straight.

I still recall your dragging up the stairs,
Allowing travel time before each bell; °
I liked your funny classes (though in truth
I really cannot claim you taught us well).

We watched you crawl from bad to worse,
Drag slower and slower until the term
You didn't walk: your classes came
To see you fade from ailing to infirm.

When you retired from teaching, as you had to
— Your body wouldn't serve your driving will —
We built a special house to cage you in
So anyone could come and see you still.

The few occasions when I looked you up
I saw a living carcass wasting slow,
That sprightliness of mind a crudish irony
When all your wretched limbs were withering so.

Without a conscious plan to be neglectful
I didn't seem to find the time
To drop in for your running commentary
On what you called "the national pantomime".

I wonder whether time has stolen from me
Something that matters deeply (or should do)
And whether anything I manage now will ever
Relieve my guilt about neglecting you.

And when you die I know I shall be sorry,
Remembering your kindness. But the fear
Of facing death stops me from coming
To see you dying smiling in your chair.

# OUTING

A rush of boys reporting in.
Enquiry, and a hush.

"Drowned, drowned, Marriott is drowned."

That curious thirst for detail swells;
in waves the teachers rise
like undertakers
and descend the cold stone steps.

# LYING IN STATE

Viewing the body endlessly
the people pass
tearfully relearning
that flesh is grass.

We're shuffling along°
(the ritual declares)
to celebrate another life.
We mask our fears.

Peering at the face of death
the people pass
fearfully relearning:
All flesh is grass.

# YOUNG WIDOW, GRAVE

A wreath of mourners
at the grave. It gapes.°
The people sing.
The service isn't meaning anything.

His secretary's legs look sleek in black.

The widow's looking farther back.
Across the gap, now flower-choked,
her swollen eyes have stumbled on
another man she lost; who poked
the fire, and when it stirred was gone.

That was another death.

# LOVE-STORY

Love gave her eyes:
the tough man snatched,
locked them up tight.

Love gave her hand:
the tough man tickled it
early one night.

Love gave her tongue:
the tough man found
it tasted right.

Love gave her body:
the tough man smiled,
switched off the light.

Love gave her heart:
the tough man fled,
flaccid with fright.

# MOTH

A somewhat intellectual moth,
she could dilate for hours on flame
and how to fight desire.
She'd read an awful lot on fire,°
but it consumed her just the same.

# WEST INDIAN LOVE-SONG
*(from England)*

The moon begat our love
the moon on the sea
You said the moon would prove
what love should be

The sea frustrates our love
dissolves my life
The moon that spun our love
sharpens the knife

And to regain my love
I'll ride the sea
I'll put my arms about the moon
and we'll be free

# DIALOGUE FOR DANCERS °
*(for the NDTC)*

### I

at home on-stage
his wife the martyr
bleeds

### II

the other woman
wraps a sensuous leg

### III

torn
between

his clinging wife's
domestic harmonies
the open breakfast face

and that sleek wanton queen
the red rose in her hair

his wanting body
writhes

# FOR A SON

Watching you swell
your mother's womb, only a crude
connection seemed to make itself.
Watching your mother swell, with having you,
taught tenderness, for she
while growing you was all my care,
happy as she rounded.
Even alive and howling clear
you seemed a thing your mother had.

But you yourself I learnt
could make me feel — maybe your laugh,
that warm primordial gurgle, did it:
your personal self enjoined my love,
tying our lives as with the living cord.

Be strong my bond and my release
from time. Be tall, stretch separate; and know
the love you've nourished though you may not care.

# LITTLE BOY CRYING

Your mouth contorting in brief spite and hurt,
your laughter metamorphosed into howls,
your frame so recently relaxed now tight
with three-year-old frustration, your bright eyes
swimming tears, splashing your bare feet,
you stand there angling for a moment's hint
of guilt or sorrow for the quick slap struck.

The ogre towers above you, that grim giant,
empty of feeling, a colossal cruel,
soon victim of the tale's conclusion, dead
at last. You hate him, you imagine
chopping clean the tree he's scrambling down
or plotting deeper pits to trap him in.

You cannot understand, not yet,
the hurt your easy tears can scald him with,
nor guess the wavering hidden behind that mask.
This fierce man longs to lift you, curb your sadness
with piggy-back or bull-fight, anything,
but dare not ruin the lessons you should learn.

You must not make a plaything of the rain.

# FAMILY PICTURES

In spite of love
desire to be alone
haunts him like prophecy.

Observe: the baby chuckles,
gurgles his delight
that daddy-man is handy,
to be stared at, clawed at,
spitted-up upon;
the baby's elder brother
laughs, or hugs, and nags
for popcorn or a pencil
or a trip.

And see: the frazzled wife
who jealously
protects the idol infant
from the smallest chance
of harm, and anxious
in the middle of the night
wakes up to coughs; and checks,
and loves, and screams
her nerves; but loves him
patient still: the wife
who sweets the bigger boy
and teases him through homework,
bright as play.

But you may not observe
(it is a private sanctuary)
the steady glowing power
that makes a man feel loved,
feel needed, all of time;
yet frees him, king of her
emotions, jockey of her
flesh, to cherish
his own corner
of the cage.

In spite of love
this dream:
to go alone
to where
the fishing boats are empty
on the beach
and no one knows
which man is
father, husband, victim,
king, the master of one cage.

# SHADOWS °

When the man taps out
a peephole in his crown,
that hole into the dark
pit is for peering down:
but it is hard to tell
what's going on down there:
when shadows thrash
and slither
what we glimpse
are figures either
wrestling for fun or
locked in combat
in a subterranean war.

# THE ROACHES

We had a home. The roaches came
to stay. They spread until they had control
of kitchen, pantry, study, then the whole
damned house. We fought them, but the game
was set. We sprayed, and they kept breeding all the same.

We found a house with plenty space,
clean and dry and full of light.
We checked beneath the sink — no roach in sight.
We checked the cupboards — not a trace
of roaches. No roach anyplace.

And so we moved.

                            The roaches came.
We sprayed, but they kept breeding all the same.

# THE FOREST

That world I knew was all too plain:
a dry world, crisp and certain
in the sun, where practically anyone
could laugh and prattle all day long,
seeing clear for seeing nothing. But

horrid those grim creatures which, obscure,
lurk in the forest where the leaves
are damp, where sun is filtered
to a nightlight feeble against fears!
Around dark tree-trunks red eyes leer:

Come; into the forest
where the leaves are damp,
where no bird sings. Come,
flee the sunlit safety of the shore.
Deep in the forest where the air is dank
embrace the gracious maggot in the mind.
The bright boat burns on the beach.

# JOURNEY INTO THE INTERIOR

Stumbling down his own oesophagus
he thought he'd check his vitals out.
He found the entrails most illegible,
it wasn't clear what innards are about.

He opted to return to air and light
and certainty; but when he tried
he found the passage blocked; so now
he spends the long day groping there, inside.

## MUSEUM PIECE °

The thing had wings
that flapped
flapped in the dark of the skull

You let it be  they said
we don't care
to know about it
you keep it  it is yours

But the thing kept going
flap
flap

So he got himself a lance
and he practised tilting
tilting

till one day when the thing went flap
he climbed on his practised horse
and galloped into the dark

He rammed the lance in its gullet
and dragged it into the light

then he wiped off the dust and the blood °
and he put it on display
(making sure to pin the wings)

# THE POND

There was this pond in the village
and little boys, he heard till he was sick,
were not allowed too near.
Unfathomable pool, they said,
that swallowed men and animals just so;
and in its depths, old people said,
swam galliwasps and nameless horrors;
bright boys kept away.

Though drawn so hard by prohibitions,
the small boy, fixed in fear, kept off;
till one wet summer, grass growing laush,
paths muddy, slippery, he found himself
there at the fabled edge.

The brooding pond was dark.
Sudden, escaping cloud, the sun
came bright; and, shimmering in guilt,
he saw his own face peering from the pool.

# NARCISSUS

They're lying; lying, all of them:
he never loved his shadow.
He saw it was another self
and tried to wring its neck.
Not love but murder on his mind,
he grappled with the other man
inside the lucid stream.

Only the surface broke.
Unblinking eyes
came swimming back in view.

At last he knew
he never would
destroy that other self.
And knowing made him shrink.

He shrank into a yellow-bellied flower.

# THE CASTLE

His mother told him of the king's
enormous thick-walled castle where
with lots of yellow courtiers
he kept his yellow court of fear.

The bold knight hopped a milk-white horse,
spurred fiercely, keen as anything;
resolved, this honourable knight,
to slay that fearful king.

The giddy knight rode hard and fast.
At dusk he heaved a dreadful sigh:
at last, that frightful yellow flag
against the darkening sky!

LIVING IS FEARING. Tired, he read
the writing on the castle wall,
and braced himself to slay that king
who terrifies us all.

The drawbridge down, the knight spurred hard,
galloping into battle;
but as he neared, the bridge pulled up
with a disdainful rattle.

Too late to stop, he took the plunge;
accoutred well, he couldn't float;
and, loud exclaiming "Death to Fear!",
he drowned himself in the moat.

# MARINERS

who are
the night-cruisers
slicing through dark
dim on the foredeck
scanning for shark

we are
the seafarers°
sick in the deep
bilious in daylight
troubled asleep

we are the sea-searchers
scaling the night
keen in the darkness
fish-eyed in light

# NOTES

These notes give details of the poems as published in the 1973 edition.

Page
8     LECTURE

9     he planted lovely seed

11     a poet, pursuing mirrors, stopped for wine

12     things in mind, hugging his white box

13     declined to share the public strain
    while struggling with his private pain.

14     to say good-bye. It may be you were right.

18     remembered and foretold

19     When he was 7, in elementary school,

20     UNIVERSITY STUDY

The window opened
on a tangled growth
of shrub, dry branches
twined in frantic strangulation.
He moved his wooden desk.

Second reel, New Life:
a barbed-wire fence
hard jagged cobblestones unworked
a solitary tree
and brown leaves
falling, falling.

He moved the damn desk back.
The old sight flicked new pain:
that semi-cultured jungle
just outside; anarchic
self-negating bush
called hedge.

He drew the curtains
and stayed in.
But all the living day
the mind's projector
played spliced re-runs:

a tree alone
self-strangled shrub
and brown leaves
falling free.

22            SATIRIST

Satirical vision:
Two clear eyes
Darting derision,
Laughing at lies.

When the eyes turn in
Will the mind dare grin?
If the eyes speak true
Will the heart laugh too?

If the eyes don't lie
Will the dry mind cry?
If the eyes see deep
Will the cold heart weep?

24      We hogged the billiard table in your room,
         We read your weekly *Mirrors* with delight;
         And if some little cretin went too far
         Your magisterial wit would put him right.

         I still recall your dragging up the stairs,
         And setting out some time before each bell;

27      As our own ends distract us
         the programmed pomp declares
         our grief is for the patriot dead.
         We calm our fears.

         But peering at the face of death

28      A wreath of mourners ring
         the grave. It gapes.

30      She'd read an awful lot on fire

32      DIALOGUE FOR THREE DANCERS
         *(for the NDTC)*

*I*

wounded
at home onstage
his wife the martyr lies
prone
arousing guilt

that other woman
regal in fading purple
wraps a sensuous leg

*II*

unmanned
in indecision he
abuses gods
who bid him choose

his clinging wife's fidelities
her tender reassuring flesh
domestic harmonies
the open breakfast face

or that sleek wanton queen
the red rose in her hair
who tightly as her loins clasp
asks nothing but a fire
to quench

*III*

balanced
in pain
his wanting body sweats

his manhood's hard

37          THE REASSURANCE

When, my sweet,
the man taps out
a peephole in his crown,
that hole into the pit's
for peering down.
But watch! — the dark forms
floundering, flapping,
slithering,
have not dethroned
the previous person

you have owned;
the person still
is what the person seems;
no pressing need to shrink
from fictive monsters
flailing at your dreams.

Bask in the present minutes:
he
uncorked by patient love
pours tonic constancy
(though pits brood fearful
since that foetid day
another man, your father,
slipped away).

Drink: and accept
the offered peephole in the mind.
You must not shrink,
no matter how the shadows thrash
or crawl.
Pull away, or blink,
and you will never
own him
all.

41          THE THING HAD WINGS

But here the thing seemed beautiful
so he wiped off the dust and the blood
and put it on display
making sure to pin the wings

45          the sea-fearers

## Some comments on Mervyn Morris's poetry.

"[His] sceptical withdrawal from sociopolitical activism, combined with his introspectiveness, has had the effect of marking Morris as the most private, the least activist in orientation of the major contemporary poets... Morris celebrates... the full exploration of each individual's private consciousness both as it reflects and exists apart from the world outside."

Lloyd Brown, *West Indian Poetry.*

"The subtle humane unity evident in *Shadowboxing* as a whole is also characteristic of many of the individual pieces... his poems continue to play in the mind."

Keith Carabine, *The Jamaica Daily News.*

"[T]ime and again, to our discomfort and delight, a Morris poem catches us. There is a lot of good, sharp sense and a lot of good, sharp fun in *Examination Centre*. Poems like springes."

Edward Baugh, *CRNLE Reviews.*

"[He is] an engraver in short sharp slashes that go deep."

Andrew Salkey, *Worlds Literature Today*

"Morris's work is unique among his contemporaries. It is not that his concerns are vastly different from theirs, but the spareness of his style... and the primacy of intellect, of poetic craft, in resolving the creative dilemma, ensure a highly characteristic signature."

Pamela Mordecai, in *Fifty Caribbean Writers* (ed. Daryl Dance).

"His poetry is well wrought without calling attention to the mechanics of its making. You come away from the poetry feeling that the creative act has brought some resolution to the numerous irreconcilable passions, conflicts and contemplations which are the subject of Morris' poetry."

Glyne Griffith, *Caribbean Review of Books.*

"Morris' poetry is distinguished by his love for signification, introspection, wit, restraint and ironic understatement. Although a very serious poet, he often demonstrates... a playfulness of tone which contributes to the endearing and enduring quality of his poetry."

Funso Aiyejina, *Trinidad and Tobago Review.*